Baby Giraffes at the Zoo

Eustacia Moldovo

Enslow Publishing
101 W. 23rd Street
Suite 240
New York, NY 10011
USA

enslow.com

Published in 2016 by Enslow Publishing, LLC.
101 W. 23rd Street, Suite 240, New York, NY 10011

Library of Congress Cataloging-in-Publication Data

Moldovo, Eustacia.
 Baby giraffes at the zoo / Eustacia Moldovo.
   pages cm. — (All about baby zoo animals)
 Audience: Age 4-6.
 Audience: K to Grade 3.
 Includes bibliographical references and index.
 Summary: "Describes the life of a giraffe calf at a zoo, including its behaviors, diet, and physical traits"—Provided by publisher.
 ISBN 978-0-7660-7084-4 (library binding)
 ISBN 978-0-7660-7081-3 (pbk.)
 ISBN 978-0-7660-7082-0 (6-pack)
 1. Giraffes—Infancy—Juvenile literature. I. Title.
 QL737.U56M65 2016
 599.63813'92—dc23
                    2015000146

Printed in the United States of America

Photo Credits: Awe Inspiring Images/Shutterstock.com, p. 16; Bryan Busovicki/Shutterstock.com, p. 8; dangdumrong/Shutterstock.com, p. 12; filo/E+/Getty Images, pp. 4–5; Henk Bentlage/Shutterstock.com, pp. 3 (right), 10, 18, 22; Jandee Jones/iStock/Thinkstock, pp. 3 (center), 20; Jody Dingle/Shutterstock.com, p. 14; MarclSchauer/Shutterstock.com, p. 1; rng/Shutterstock.com, pp. 3 (left), 6.

Cover Credits: rng/Shutterstock.com (giraffe calf in zoo); Nelson Marques/Shutterstock.com (baby blocks on spine).

Contents

Words to Know...................... 3

Who Lives at the Zoo? 5

Read More 24

Web Sites 24

Index 24

Words to Know

| calf | nap | patch |

Who lives at the zoo?

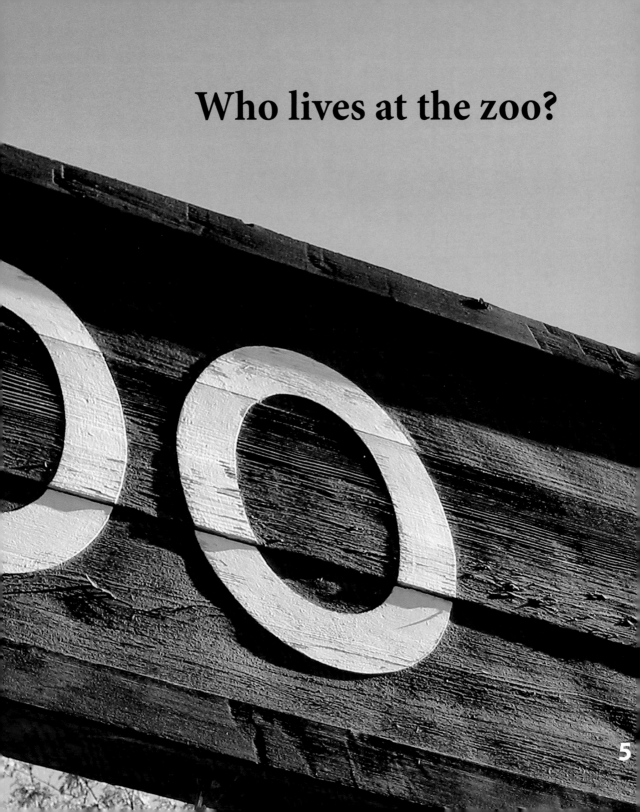

A baby giraffe lives at the zoo!

A baby giraffe is called a calf.

Giraffe calves are tan with brown patches. Their fur has a strong smell that keeps bugs away.

A giraffe calf has a long, dark tongue. This helps it grab food and clean itself.

A giraffe calf has a long neck. This helps it reach leaves and twigs from the tops of trees.

A giraffe calf has two furry horns on its head. They are bigger on male giraffes.

A giraffe calf lives with its mother at the zoo. The mother calls her baby to her by making a loud, deep sound.

A giraffe calf takes short naps. It does not sleep all night like people do.

You can see a giraffe calf at the zoo!

Read More

Amstutz, Lisa J. *Giraffes Are Awesome!* Mankato, Minn.: Capstone Press, 2015.

Glaser, Rebecca Stromstad. *Giraffes*. Minneapolis, Minn.: Bullfrog Books, 2013.

Web Sites

National Geographic: Giraffe
kids.nationalgeographic.com/content/kids/en_US/animals/giraffe/

San Diego Zoo: Giraffe
kids.sandiegozoo.org/animals/mammals/giraffe

Index

calf, 9, 11, 13, 15, 17, 19, 21, 23

food, 13

fur, 11, 17

horns, 17

mother, 19

naps, 21

neck, 15

patches, 11

sound, 19

tongue, 13

trees, 15

zoo, 5, 7, 19, 23

Guided Reading Level: D
Guided Reading Leveling System is based on the guidelines recommended by Fountas and Pinnell.

Word Count: 134